African Magic Series

COOKING FOR THE ORISHAS

MONIQUE JOINER SIEDLAK

Oshun
Publications

©2017 Monique Joiner Siedlak

All rights reserved. This book or parts thereof may not be reproduced in any form, stored in any retrieval system, or transmitted in any form by any means—electronic, mechanical, photocopy, recording, or otherwise—without prior written permission of the publisher, except as provided by United States of America copyright law.

Second Edition 2018

ISBN: 978-1-948834-71-1

Publisher

www.oshunpublications.com

Disclaimer

All the material contained in this book is provided for educational and informational purposes only. No responsibility can be taken for any results or outcomes resulting from the use of this material. While every attempt has been made to provide information that is both accurate and effective, the author does not assume any responsibility for the accuracy or use/misuse of this information.

Cover design by Monique Joiner Siedlak

Cover image by Pixabay.com

Logo design by Monique Joiner Siedlak

Logo image by Pixabay.com

Other Books in the Series

African Spirituality Beliefs and Practices

Hoodoo

Seven African Powers: The Orishas

Want to learn about African Magic, Wicca, or even Reiki while cleaning your home, exercising, or driving to work? I know it's tough these days to simply find the time to relax and curl up with a good book. This is why I'm delighted to share that I have books available in audiobook format.

Best of all, you can get the audiobook version of this book or any other book by me for free as part of a 30-day Audible trial.

Members get free audiobooks every month and exclusive discounts. It's an excellent way to explore and determine if audiobook learning works for you.

If you're not satisfied, you can cancel anytime within the trial period. You won't be charged, and you can still keep your book. To choose your free audiobook, visit:

www.mojosiedlak.com/free-audiobooks

WANT UPDATES,
FREEBIES & GIVEAWAYS?!
MONIQUE JOINER SIEDLAK
THE
ORISHAS
JOIN MY
NEWSLETTER!
mojosiedlak.com/newsletter-signup

Contents

Introduction

Yoruba deities are called orishas, a terminology that you're already quite familiar with by this point. However, the word "deity" is perhaps not the best to describe the orishas. They are not your typical supernatural beings with fearful powers but rather complex concepts that link people, objects, and special powers alike. The Yoruba people believe that an orisha is born when two elements collide: the divine power to make things happen and a natural force/divine ancestor/an object that is a witness and supporter of said changes. It's a bit hard to wrap the head around this definition, right?

Besides referring to deities, the Yoruba people use the term "orisha" when talking about the head. They believe that a person has an ori (the anatomical head that we have) and an ori-inu (the internal head, which holds a person's spirit and personality). The ori-inu is considered to be given by the supreme god, and it determines someone's character and destiny. In the traditional Yoruba belief, the most valuable of riches is having a good head (referring to both a good mind and a good personality).

Orishas are the negotiators between the world of the humans and the supreme deity. Orishas are similar in role to the Catholic saints, but they are very human in nature. They are not an embodiment of perfection, but rather one of good and bad characteristics. They can make mistakes and misbehave. Orishas live on Earth as divine spirits, humans that ascended to divinities, or as natural elements (mountains, rivers, trees). Yoruba people also associate mundane things like numbers or pieces of clothing with specific orishas, leaving way for a whole realm of codes and messages ready to be interpreted. There are over 3,000 orishas, all of which are said to be just incarnations of the divine being Olodumare.

Creating Changes

Produce positive change in your life. While you experiment with specialties from around the Scattered Afro world

Cooking for the Orishas is not a simple task, as each one has specific preferences regarding food that he or she accepts and preparation. The cook must be well versed in these divine preferences for not committing any violation of these taboos.

Individuals are offended by animal sacrifices, in Western countries, particularly when deceased remains of animals are exposed in communities and added public places. So now, there are fewer of these manners of ritual. To be more acceptable, particular in America, Santeria has made this part of its effort.

Similar to their followers, the Orishas have their favorite foods and are tremendously delighted to have them given as offerings.

The cook should follow several adherences. In addition to familiarity and attentiveness, the cook must in addition practice immaculate hygiene. Cleanness is vital. Shower as soon as you get out of bed and before entering the kitchen. You want to have your hair up, if it is long and keep your hands and nails above all clean.

The kitchen should be impeccable. Inspect the kitchen to make certain you have everything you need. Take in account the cleaning supplies such as detergents, paper towels, dishtowels and sponges. You really do not want to run to the store once you have begun.

In addition, every time you take a pot or casserole pan, you should make sure it is clean. You want to have a different spoon for each food to stir with and not to let them mix. Not only is it wrong it is dangerous to get the spoon used to stir one food and use it to stir another. The Orishas have their taboos.

In perfect conditions, there would be cooking and serving tools for each Orisha Each Orisha has their own plates, bowls, pans, cups, cutlery, ladles, tongs and other kitchen utensils.

Bon Appetit!

ONE

Orishas Traditional Foods Ingredients

Having the correct ingredients are just as important as the dish you are creating. Here are the basics to get you going.

Note: Not all items listed are used in recipes in this book.

GRAINS, Rice and Pasta

Corn Meal
Rice
White Hominy
Yellow Hominy
Baking Essentials
Sugar
Honey
Corn Starch
Molasses
Sugar Cane Syrup
Roasted Corn Flour
Wheat Flour
Condensed Milk
Evaporated Milk
Raisins

. . .

Herbs and Spices

Salt
Black Pepper
Cinnamon
Oregano
Parsley
Achiote
Saffron

LEGUMES, Nuts and Seeds

Black Beans
Black Eyed Peas
Chick Peas
Kidney Beans
Red Pinto Beans

OILS, Sauces and Vinegars

Tomato Sauce
Dry Cooking Wine
Cooking Sherry
Olive Oil
Vegetable Oil
Palm Oil
Lard
Coconut Oil
Cocoa Butter

VEGETABLES, Fruits, Herbs

Corn
Cilantro

Green Peppers
Red Peppers
Onions
Raisins
Malanga
Pumpkin
Yams
Garlic
Ginger
Star Anise
Coconuts
Collard Greens
Plantains
Plantain Leaves
White Yams
White Sweet Potatoes
Chili Peppers
Yucca
Okra

Dairy

Milk
Eggs

MEATS

Beef
Pork
Salted Beef
Short Ribs
Seafood
Fish
Shrimp

TWO

Elegua

Other Names: Elegba, Legba, Papa Legba.

Elegua represents the beginning and end of life as well as the opener and closer of paths in life. He is a powerful orisha that is often depicted as either a young child or a very old man. His signature colors are red and black, his symbolic number is 3 (and any multiplier of 3), and his day of the week is Monday.

Elegua's favorite offerings are toys (kites, toy soldiers, and balls), candy, keys, silver coins, straw hats, cigars, and some very specific foods (coconuts, toasted corn, smoked fish, red palm oil, white cooking wine). On Mondays, it is advised to make an offering to Elegua to gain the favor of the orisha. Except for pigeon; Elegua will eat pretty much anything for offerings.

Popcorn for Elegua

Ingredients:

Loose Kernel Popcorn
Palm Oil
Dash of Smoked Dried Fish

Directions:

Cook loose kernel popcorn according to the package Directions: using palm oil as your preferred cooking oil. Once the popcorn is cooked, serve it in a bowl with a dash of smoked dried fish on top next to Elegua's shrine for a suitable length of time. At that point, remove and discard naturally as recommended by means of understanding.

Carmel Popcorn Balls

Ingredients:

10 cups Popped Popcorn
1 1/2 cups Brown Sugar
1 cup Light Corn Syrup
1 cup Water
1/2 cup White Sugar
1/2 teaspoon Salt
1/2 cup Butter
2 teaspoons White Vinegar

Directions:

In large bowl Place popped corn. Mix syrup, brown sugar, white sugar, water, vinegar and salt in a saucepan. Heat to boiling stirring frequently over medium high heat. When it starts boiling stir continuously until a small quantity of mixture when dropped into very cold water, creates a ball. Decrease heat to low and stir in butter until it is melted. Pour syrup over popcorn in bowl, while stirring until well coated. Allow cool slightly. With buttered hands, shape popcorn into balls. Makes about 12 balls.

Peppered Gizzards for Elegua, Ogun and Ochosi

Ingredients:

2 packs Gizzard
3 Habanero Pepper

2 fresh Tomatoes
½ large Onion
½ cup water
1 large Red Pepper
3 tablespoons Vegetable Oil
2 Maggi Cubes
1 teaspoon Curry Powder
½ teaspoon Salt
½ teaspoon Thyme
½ teaspoon Salt

Directions:

Rinse and place the gizzard in a medium sized pot. Add in ½ cup water, 1 cube of Maggi and ½ teaspoon of salt. Simmer on low heat for 25 minutes. Place another pot on medium heat adding in oil, tomatoes, onion, Habanero pepper and red pepper. Mix and cover allowing simmering for approximately 15 minutes.

Remove gizzards from heat, discarding excess fluid. Add the cooked gizzard into the pepper sauce. Add in curry, bay leaf and thyme. Cover and simmer for another 15 minutes.

Note: Instead of frying Gizzards, you can fry or bake before adding to the sauce.

Coffee for Elegua

Ingredients:

½ liter Hot Water
3 heaping teaspoons finely Ground Coffee
10 teaspoons of Honey or Sugar
1 teaspoon Cinnamon
¼ teaspoon Allspice
¼ teaspoon Ginger
1 clove or a pinch Ground Cloves
½ cup optional Coconut Milk or Cream

Directions:

In a saucepan, you will place in all of the ingredient excluding the coconut milk or cream. While greeting Eshu, Turn on the heat, with the name for your thanks or needs. Roast for a very short time while stirring the ingredients in a multiple of three. If using sugar, it will just start to melt, honey, will melt to a thinner liquid. Continue stirring while slowly pouring in the water. Aim to stir it clockwise a multiple of three times.

When all the water is in, stop stirring and at that point let it start to foam. You do not want the coffee to burn, so you may need to turn the heat down. When it is foaming, stir from the top to stop it.

When it settles down, stop and let it foam again. At that point, stir from the top again. Perform this once more for three times. Turn off the heat, and move the pot allowing it settle.

Without using a strainer, careful to get as little of the solids as possible into a cup, pour the coffee. At this point, you can add the coconut milk or cream if you like.

Elegua Gingerbread Cookies

Ingredients:

3 cups All-Purpose Flour
2/3 cup unsulfured Molasses
½ cup packed Light Brown Sugar
¼ cup room temperature Vegetable Shortening
1 large Egg
1 stick room temperature Unsalted Butter
1 teaspoon Baking Soda
¾ teaspoon Ground Cinnamon
¾ teaspoon Ground Ginger
½ teaspoon Ground Allspice
½ teaspoon Ground Cloves
½ teaspoon Salt

¼ teaspoon freshly Ground Black Pepper

Directions:

Preheat oven to 350 degrees F, position the racks in the top, and bottom thirds of the oven

Sift the flour, ginger, allspice, cloves, baking soda, cinnamon, salt and pepper through a sieve into a medium bowl. Set to the side.

Using a hand-held electric mixer at high speed, beat the butter and vegetable shortening in a large bowl until well combined. Add the brown sugar and beat until the mixture is light in consistency and color. Beat in the egg and molasses. Gradually using a wooden spoon, mix in the flour mixture to create a stiff dough. Divide the dough into two parts and wrap each one in plastic wrap. Refrigerate until chilled, which should take about 3 hours. Keeping one part refrigerated, roll out the dough, and work with one part at a time. Take out the dough from the refrigerator and allow it to stand at room temperature until just sufficiently warm enough to roll out without cracking, Set the dough on a lightly floured work surface and sprinkle the top of the dough with flour. Roll out the dough approximately 1/8 inch thick, making sure that the dough is not sticking to the work surface. Roll out slightly thicker for softer cookies. With cookie cutters, cut out the cookies and move, placing the cookies 1 inch apart, on a nonstick cookie sheets. Lightly knead the leftovers together and form into another ball. Cover and refrigerate for 5 minutes before rolling out again to cut out more cookies.

Switching the positions of the cookies, bake from top to bottom and back to front midway through baking, 10 to 12 minutes, until the edges of the cookies are set and crisp. Allow to cool on the sheets for 5 minutes, and then move to wire racks to cool completely. Makes about 36 3 inch cookies.

THREE

Yemaya

Other Names: La Sirene, Mommi, Nana Buruku, Iemanja, Iemaia, Yemalla, Yemanja, Yemoja, Yemonja, Yemeya.

Yemaya is the goddess of the oceans and the spiritual mother of all the orishas. Her name translates to "mother whose children are the fish," and she is widely referred to as the Mother Goddess or "mama watta" (mother of all the waters). She is the protector of all mothers and pregnant women, as well as the guardian of the Ogun River (the largest river of Yorubaland).

According to Yoruba myths, Yemoja is a primordial orisha who assisted Obatala in creating the world. She, alongside 16 other orishas, prepared the world for humankind, and she serves as the counterpart for Olokun (who represents spite and the unknown). Yemoja is commonly portrayed as the wife of various male orishas such as Obatala and as the mother of Chango, Oya, Oshun, Ogun, and many other orishas (if not all). However, some sources describe her as only taking on the role of the mother and not actually giving birth.

In most myths about Yemoja, she is defined by her motherly nature as well as her sensitivity and shyness. For example, whenever she is insulted by other orishas, she turns herself into a river. Yet, the soothing mother can become violent at the flip of a switch if her children are in danger. Because she is an embodiment of all bodies of water, Yemoja is also considered the protector of sailors, fishermen, swimmers, dockworkers, and all people who work or travel around water. Sacred stones called otas are placed in rivers and bodies of water all around Africa to honor Yemoja.

Yemoja's popularity saw a major rise during the slave era when the Yoruba people were captured and forced to work for white men. People prayed to Yemoja to ease their sufferings, protect those that were lost, and give them comfort and hope. During these times when the Yoruba people were not allowed to practice their own religious beliefs, Yemoja was worshiped under the guise of the Virgin Mary.

Yemoja's totem animals are the snail, the duck, the vulture, and the snake. Her altars are usually decorated with symbols of the sea such as seashells, miniature boats, fountains with fish, fishnets, blue and white pottery, and peacock feathers. Her symbolic number is 7 (representing the seven seas), and she is often portrayed as wearing skirts with seven blue and white layers. Yemoja's devotees wear seven silver bracelets and an ileke (necklace) with seven beads (turquoise and clear quartz beads or clear and blue crystal beads) as protection tokens. The ileke is most commonly worn by pregnant women to protect their unborn children. Some of Yemoja's followers wear a specific fish-gill facial marking as a tribute to the mother goddess.

Yemoja accepts animal sacrifices (lamb, rooster, duck, fish, pigeon, goat, and ram) but also small offerings such as seashells, coral, turquoise, silver keys, and decorative anchors. The Yoruba people believe that Yemoja can be summoned with a gourd rattle.

Interesting facts:

- Yemoja is credited with ending the cruel practice of twin infanticide in the West African world.

• She is the patron goddess of the Gelade Society (Society of Mothers), a fertility organization with an important role in the annual Gelade Festival.

• Some depictions show Yemoja as a half-fish hybrid resembling a mermaid.

Yemaya enjoys rich and delicious foods, such as guinea hen, rooster, and ram that she shares with Chango as well as fish, cantaloupe, berries, watermelon and coconut.

Yemaya's Sweet Three Milk Cake

Ingredients:

2 cups Whole Milk

1 ½ cups All-Purpose Flour

2 cups White Sugar (split as 1 cup and 1 cup)

1 teaspoon Baking Powder

½ cup Margarine or Unsalted Butter

5 Eggs

1 ½ teaspoon Vanilla Extract (split as 1 teaspoon and ½ teaspoon)

1 14 ounce can Sweetened Condensed Milk

1 12 fluid ounce can Evaporated Milk

1 ½ cups Heavy Whipping Cream

9x13 inch Baking Pan

Baking Spray

Directions:

Preheat oven to 350 degrees F.

Grease and flour your 9x13 inch baking pan. Sift flour and baking powder together and set aside. Cream margarine or butter and one cup sugar together until fluffy. Add the eggs and the ½ teaspoon vanilla extract. Beat mixture well.

Add the flour mixture to your butter mixture 2 tablespoons at a time; mix until well blended. Pour batter into prepared sprayed pan. Bake at 350 degrees F for 30 minutes. Prick cake a number of times with a fork.

Combine the margarine, whole milk, and evaporated milk together. Pour over the top of the cooled cake.

Whip the whipping cream, the left over 1 cup of the sugar, and the remaining 1 teaspoon vanilla together until thick and Spread on the top of cake. Be sure to keep the cake refrigerated.

Yemaya Coconut Fish

Ingredients:

1 pound Whitefish Fillets
½ cup Dry Bread Crumbs
¼ cup Chopped Mixed Nuts
¼ cup Shredded Coconut
¼ cup Prepared Brown Mustard
¼ cup Mayonnaise
1 teaspoon Granulated Sugar
1 teaspoon Salt
½ teaspoon Cayenne Pepper
Cooking spray
Small Bowl
Medium bowl
Medium Baking Dish

Directions:

Preheat oven to 375 degrees F.

Lightly grease a medium baking dish. Mix brown mustard and mayonnaise in a small bowl. Mix in a medium bowl, shredded coconut, chopped mixed nuts, dry breadcrumbs, cayenne pepper, sugar, and salt.

Dip fish in the mustard mixture in the small bowl, followed by the breadcrumb mixture in the medium bowl. Position coated fish fillets in the prepared medium baking dish. Bake for 20 minutes or until fish can be easily flaked with a fork.

Yemaya Coconut Rice

Ingredients:

2 cup Rice
2 cup Coconut Water
1 cup Coconut Milk
1 cup Water
1 tablespoon Butter
1 teaspoon Salt

Directions:

With cold water, rinse and drain rice. Place in a saucepan with coconut milk, water, and salt. Set the pot on high heat and bring to a boil. Stir while reducing the heat to the lowest possible position and cover the pot with the lid. Continue cooking for 15 minutes. Remove the pot from the stove and allow to stand covered for 10 minutes. Fluff up with fork and serve.

Olele

Ingredients:

1 pound Black-Eyed Peas
1 small Onion
2 cloves of Garlic
2 tablespoons Oil
Salt and Pepper

Directions:

Immerse peas in hot water, remove shells and place in cold water for 10-15 minutes. Pour off water and mash peas. Chop and sauté garlic and onion, mixing in peas.

Place three tablespoon of the mix into shells made from aluminum foil. Set shells in a double boiler over a medium flame for one hour

Serve hot and season to taste.

FOUR

Chango

Other Names: Shango, Xango.

Chango is the orisha of thunder and lightning, and he is believed to be both a deified Oyo king and a personified natural force. As a mortal, Shango was the fourth king of the village of Oyo. Stories describe him as powerful, with a thunderous voice and the ability to spew fire, but they also characterize him as being unfair and cowardly. When a minister challenged Shango for the throne, he fled into a forest where he met his demise at his own hands. After his death, the houses of his enemies were set on fire. The Yoruba people saw that as a sign that Shango ascended to divinity and took his revenge. The worship of Shango thus became central to the political world of Oyo.

Shango is often depicted as having an oshe (double-headed ax) emerging from his head, which symbolizes a thunderbolt. Priests hold an oshe while dancing or conducting rituals to honor the great orisha. Shango's devotees also play the bata drums, which they believe Shango uses to conjure up storms.

During the European slave trade, Shango became a symbol of resistance for the enslaved Yoruba people. His followers are said to have great powers and are graced with self-control.

Chango offerings consist of apples, corn bread, okra, and tobacco, hot/spicy foods such as chili peppers and tamales as well as red wine dry.

Chango's Okra Stew

Ingredients:

1 pound Okra
1 large Onion
1 large Green Pepper
1/2 cup Water
1/4 cup Red Pepper
1/4 teaspoon Black Pepper
1/4 teaspoon Salt
Oil

Directions:

Boil okra till tender but do not overcook. Sauté onion, green pepper, onion and red pepper in oil add salt and pepper add okra and simmer. Serve over Eba.

Eba

Ingredients:

4 cups water
2 cups Cassava Flour (Garri)

Directions:

Bring the water to a boil in a large pot. Sprinkle in the cassava flour, and cook, stirring constantly, until it becomes a paste similar to mashed potato consistency.

Chango's Baked Apples

Ingredients:

3 large Baking Apples
½ cup Water
1/3 cup Sugar
3 tablespoon Butter
½ teaspoon Ground Nutmeg
½ teaspoon Ground Cinnamon
Red Hots Cinnamon Candies

Directions:

Preheat oven to 350 degrees F.

Core apples and place in an ungreased 2-qt. baking dish. Put about 1 ½ teaspoons of butter in the middle of each apple hole. Combine the sugar, nutmeg and cinnamon and sprinkle mixture on top of the butter in the hole along with the top of the apple.

Bake, uncovered for 30-35 minutes or until apples are tender. After the apples have been baking about 15 to 20 minutes, place one or two Red Hot cinnamon candy in the middle of each apple. Let stand 15 minutes before serving.

To Petition Chango

Ingredients:

Cornmeal
Cut Okra
Corojo Butter or Palm Oil
Tomato Paste
Salt
6 Small Bowls

Directions:

Bring a pot of water to a boil and cook the cornmeal until it becomes thick. Remove from stove. Add the cut okras into the pot of cornmeal stirring well. Add tomato paste and a little bit of salt for taste. Lastly, add corojo butter or palm oil and mix all together. Place back on stove and Bring back to a boil. Once everything is cooked remove from stove and divide the mixture into your six bowls. Take these bowls to a park or any area where there are plenty of palm trees. Set each bowl by six different palm trees while petitioning to Chango. If you reside in an area that does not have palm trees, you can take them to a wooded area and leave all of them around a tall tree. Once you return home, light a candle for Chango.

Ogbono Soup

Ingredients:

2 pounds Assortment of Meats Ham Hocks, Oxtail, Pigs Feet Tripe, etc.

1 pound pre-soaked Fish

1 pound washed Dried Fish

½ pound cleaned whole Dry Prawns

½ pound Ground Ogbono Seeds

½ pound Ground Crayfish

½ ground Pepper

1 medium Onion

10 ounce Palm Oil

3 Maggi Cubes

Water

Salt

Directions:

Washed the assortment of meats completely and place in a pot. Add the sliced onions, ground pepper, Maggi cubes and some water. Cook for 30 minutes.

Add the washed smoked fish and stock of fish, cook for another 10-15 minutes adding a drop of water as needed to keep it from burning. Place to side when done.

Heat the oil and fry the ground seeds for 3 minutes to bring out the nutty flavor. Stir to dissolve the ogbono in the oil. When all the ogbono powder is completed mixed with the oil. Set the heat of your stove to low and start stirring. You will notice the ogbono start to thicken and draw.

Keep stirring until the ogbono has completely absorbed the meat stock.

Add a small quantity of the hot water and stir until the ogbono has absorbed all the water. Repeat this process until you get a consistency that you desire

Making sure that your heat is set to low, cover the pot and start cooking. Once it starts to simmer, stir every 2 to 3 minutes for 20 minutes to avoid the ogbono sticking to the base of the pot.

Add the meat, pepper, ground crayfish, prawns and salt to taste. The ogbono may have become thicker from the cooking. If so, add a little bit more water and stir very well. Then cover and cook until done. Allow to simmer for another 10 minutes, check seasoning and serve hot with mashed yam.

Note: For a different flavor, you can also add mushroom and Okra.

FIVE

Obatala

Other Names: Osala, Oshala, Orisala, Orishala.

Obatala is known to be a wise Orisha and is usually identified as the chief and judge. He is married to Yemaya, who is the mother figure of all Orishas and the Goddess of the Oceans.

According to some patakis, Obatala is the father of all human beings. He and Yemaya created many children. One day he got very drunk while making humans because he was thirsty and drank some palm wine. Under the influence of the wine, he made some malformed humans.

Once he sobered up, he realized what he had done. He vowed from that day that he would never drink, and now every handicapped or deformed person has a special place in his heart. He takes extra care of them.

Obatala shows mercy and compassion because he realizes that he erred once he got drunk on the palm wine. This is why he is also known to be the fairest Orisha of all.

Obatala offerings consists of Black eyed Peas, the meat or the milk of a coconut, eggs, rice, mushrooms, potatoes, milk, water.

Soursop and Rice Pudding

Ingredients:

1 ½ cups Cooked Rice

1 cup Soursop Pulp Strained and Sweetened to taste

1 cup Whole Milk

½ cup Heavy Cream

1/3 cups Sugar

1 beaten Egg

¼cups White Raisins

1 tablespoon Unsalted Butter

½ teaspoon Vanilla

¼ teaspoon Nutmeg

Directions:

Mix rice, soursop, whole milk, and sugar in saucepan. Cook over medium heat. Stir occasionally until it becomes thick and creamy. Blend heavy cream and egg. Stir into rice mixture. Add raisins. Cook for 2 minutes longer, stirring occasionally. Add butter, vanilla and nutmeg. Spoon this into serving dishes.

White Rice with Eggs

Ingredients:

4 White Eggs

1 cup Long-Grain White Rice

1 ½ cups Water

½ teaspoon Salt

Cocoa Butter

Powdered Eggshells (for Obatala)

Directions:

Place your eggs in a saucepan and cover with cold water by 1 inch. Over a medium-high heat, bring water to a boil and cover. Remove from the heat and set aside 8 to 10 minutes. Drain water, cool eggs in ice water and peel.

In a separate saucepan with a lid, combine rice, salt and water (omit salt if for Obatala) and bring to a boil. Stirring only once, cover and reduce to low heat. Cook for 15 to18 minutes. While cooking, do not raise the lid or stir. Remove from heat and allow to sit, covered, for 5 minutes. Fluff with a fork.

Once the rice is done cooking, chop up some cocoa butter over the hot rice and stir it in so it melts and coats the grains of rice. Plate the rice in a tall mound or tower on a white plate. Cut the four eggs lengthwise and arrange them around the edge of the mound of rice.

Note: For Obatala, do not use salt. Not in the eggs, not in the rice. Top the rice and eggs with a sprinkle of more cocoa butter and a sprinkling of powdered eggshells. Place the rice beside Obatala's shrine for a suitable length of time. At that point, remove and discard naturally as recommended by means of understanding.

Meringue Cookies for Obatala

Ingredients:

3 large Egg Whites
¾ cup Granulated White Sugar
¼ teaspoon Cream of Tartar
¼ teaspoon Pure Vanilla Extract
Shaved Almonds

Directions:

Preheat oven to 200 degrees F, placing the rack in the center of the oven. Line a baking sheet with parchment paper.

Add sugar to Processor and pulse on and off until fine about 30-60 Seconds. Using an electric mixer, with the whisk attachment, beat the egg whites, in the bowl, on low-medium speed until frothy. Add the cream of tartar and keep beating the whites until they hold soft peaks. Put in the sugar, a little at a time, and continue to beat mixture, on medium-high speed, until the meringue maintains very stiff peaks. Blend in the vanilla extract.

You will know when the meringue is done. If it maintains stiff peaks, you rub a little between your thumb, and index finger it does not feel gritty, it is done.

Fill a pastry bag fitted with a ½-inch tip with the meringue. Pipe 2 ½-inch rounds of meringue cookies in rows on the prepared baking sheet. Sprinkle the tops of the cookies with a few shaved almonds.

Bake the meringue cookies for approximately 1 ½ to 1 ¾ hours, turning the baking sheet from front to back half way through baking to make sure of even baking. The meringues cookies are done when they are pale in color and crisp. Opening the door a crack, turn off the oven and leave the meringue cookies in the oven to complete their drying for several hours. The meringue cookies can be covered and stored at room temperature for several days.

Makes about 10 - 2 ½ inch meringues

For Obatala

Stack these into a tower on a white plate and present these to Obatala for the necessary amount of time as prescribed by divination. Remove the meringue after a suitable length of time. At that point, discard naturally as recommended by means of understanding.

SIX

Ogun

Other Names: Oggun, Ogou Ogum.

Ogun is the orisha of war and iron. Stories present him as one of the first orishas to even come down to earth. Myths say that Ogun saw that the endless forests were not suitable for humans to live in. So, with advice from Orunmila, the wise sage orisha, he learned how to use iron and create tools that could chop down the trees. Ogun later taught the other orishas and the humans how to forge iron into powerful tools (axes, hunting tools, weapons, plows) that made life easier.

Ogun is seen as a kind god who loves justice. However, he is also prone to making mistakes. It is said that before a battle that took place a long time ago, he drank palm wine. This made him rather confused and led to him slaying his own people. Ashamed of himself, the god sunk into the ground to mourn the loss of innocent lives. But the Yoruba people have forgiven Ogun, and his popularity hasn't dwindled, especially since he is seen as a symbol of freedom and victory.

The orisha is usually portrayed as a muscular man with a sword in his hands and an iron cauldron nearby—the poster figure of the blacksmith warrior. Ogun's color is red, and his favorite offerings are rum and spicy foods. Back in the day, people would sacrifice dogs in his name, but modern worshipers prefer to sacrifice roosters, rats, and black snakes.

Ogun's food offerings are typically meat, nuts, chili, peppers, hot and spicy foods roots and soda crackers with palm oil, rum, and whiskey.

Ogun's Creamy Potato Pork Chops

Ingredients:

6 pork chops
1 20 ounce package Frozen Hash Brown Potatoes, thawed
1 10.75 ounce can Condensed Cream of Celery Soup
1 ½ cups French-Fried Onions, to be divided
1 cup shredded Cheddar cheese, to be divided
½ cup Milk
½ cup Sour Cream
1 tablespoon Vegetable Oil
Salt and Pepper to taste
Large Skillet
Medium Bowl
9x13 inch Baking Dish

Directions:

Preheat oven to 350 degrees F.

In a large skillet, heat oil over medium high heat. Add pork chops and sauté until browned. Remove from skillet and place on paper towel to drain.

Mix in a medium bowl, condensed soup, sour cream, milk, salt and pepper. Stir in potatoes, ½ cup onions and ½ cup cheese. Combine together and spread mixture on the bottom of baking dish. Position pork chops over the potato mixture.

Cover the dish and bake for about 40 minutes, or up to inside temperature of the pork has reached 145 degrees F. Remove the cover; top with remaining onions and cheese then continue to bake uncovered for five more minutes.

Ogun Soup

Ingredients:

½ pound chopped Boneless Chicken or Ground Beef
1 large chopped Onion
1 chopped Potato
1 chopped Carrot
½ cup chopped Mushrooms
1 cup chopped Dandelion Leaves
1 teaspoon Annatto
Salt

Directions:

Fry the meat and onion until the meat is slightly browned. Then add the herbs and sauté for a minute or two, adding the water, annatto, potato and carrot. Bring to a boil, and then turn the heat down to low. After about 2 hours of low heat, when it is fully cooked, blend in a food processor.

Serve to Ogun; it must be between warm and hot.

Deep Fried Black Eyed Peas

Ingredients:

1 pound dried Black-Eyed Peas
1 seeded and diced Jalapeno Pepper
1 largely diced Onion
2 Bay Leaves
2 teaspoons Seafood Seasoning
½ teaspoon Salt
Canola Oil

Directions:

After sorting and rinsing, place the black-eyed peas into a large container and cover with several inches of cool water. Allow to sit 8 hours or overnight.

Drain and rinse the black-eyed peas. Add in enough water to cover the peas by about 3 inches. Add the onion, jalapeno pepper and bay leaves. Bring to a boil. Reduce heat to low, and continue to simmer 40 to 50 minutes or until the black-eyed peas are tender. Do not allow them to get mushy. If needed, add more water to keep the black-eyed peas covered while cooking. Drain water off using a colander. Toss bay leaves.

Heat the oil in a large saucepan or deep fryer. With care, pour about 1 cup of mixture at a time into the hot oil and fry 4 to 7 minutes until crisp. Remove from oil and drain on paper towels. Mix the hot peas in a bowl with the seafood seasoning and salt. Serve hot.

SEVEN

Oya

Other Names: Iansa Yansa, Yansan.

Oya is the orisha of weather, especially that of destructive phenomena such as rainstorms, tornadoes, and hurricanes. This deity, who is fond of destruction, is Shango's favorite wife and a representation of strong female leadership. She is also an orisha of change, a protector of the Niger River, and a powerful warrior ready to fight for what she believes to be right.

Her sacred number is 9, and she is often depicted as having nine whirlwinds surrounding her. She fancies the colors white, purple, deep red, and orange, and she is frequently portrayed wearing a twisted turban that mimics the appearance of buffalo horns. When threatened, Oya has the ability to turn into a water buffalo. Her symbols are the sword, the machete, and the fly whisk, which are very fitting with her warrior spirit.

Many believe Oya to be in charge of the winds of change, so they call upon her when they need guidance. Similarly, Oya is seen as a fierce protector of women who helps them out in times of need. However, Oya is a tough, temperamental mother who can always resort to violence and chaos. So, she is both loved and feared.

Oya's favorite offerings are grapes, spicy food, eggplants, rum, gin, wine, fruits, and fish. To honor Oya, one should wear brightly colored garments, copper jewelry (with red stones), and decorate her altar with masks, swords, wind instruments, and buffalo horns.

Fried Eggplant

Ingredients:

1 whole medium to large sized Eggplant
2 cups Cornmeal
1 Egg lightly beaten with a little water
Kosher or Sea Salt
Pepper
Paprika
Palm Oil

Directions:

Peel and slice eggplant about 3/8 inch thick. Lay the eggplant in a colander and sprinkle them with salt. Make sure each eggplant round has a thin sprinkling of salt on it. Allow the slices sit for 20-30 minutes until drops of liquid form on the top.

Rinse the eggplant pieces to eliminate the salt. Tap dry and place on a cutting board. Sprinkle the slices lightly with black pepper. Dip each slice of eggplant into the beaten egg then coat in the cornmeal and coat completely.

Heat ¼ inch of palm oil in a cast iron skillet over medium until it is hot enough for frying. Place three slices gradually into the hot oil. Allow the slices to fry for 2-3 minutes. When they just begin to get brown and tender on the bottom, flip and repeat on the other side until cooked through. Remove slices from the hot oil and drain on a paper towel or drying rack.

Akara

Ingredients:

½ pound dried Black-Eyed Peas
2 Onions
2 Ripe Tomatoes
1 Green Pepper
1 finely chopped Red Pepper or Hot Chile Pepper
¼ cup chopped Parsley Leaves
Salt
Ground White Pepper
Olive Oil

Directions:

With running water, clean the black-eyed peas. Allow them to soak in water for at least a few hours. Overnight would be better. Following soaking them, massage them together between your hands to get rid of the skins. Rinse to wash away the skins as well as any other remains. Drain in a colander.

Using a processor, coarsely chop the onion and red pepper. Add the saturated peas and puree ingredients to a paste. Move to a bowl and, whisk the mixture, using a whisk, while adding white pepper, salt and just a little liquid left behind.

Make fritters by scooping up a spoon full of batter using an ice cream scoop, form into balls about the size of a golf ball.

Drop into a pot of hot olive oil, heated to 360 degrees F. Fry until golden brown. Remove to paper towel-lined plate. Season again with salt and pepper.

Serve as a side dish, snack, or an appetizer.

Note: If the Akara fall apart in the oil, stir in some crushed breadcrumbs, cornmeal or a beaten egg.

Variation: Add a half cup of finely chopped leftover cooked meat or dried shrimp to the batter before frying.

EIGHT

Oshun

Other Names: Ochun, Oxum, Osun.

Oshun is the orisha of rivers, and she is considered to be one of the most powerful Yoruba deities and is associated with love, sensuality, purity, and water. Oshun is frequently depicted as a beautiful woman wearing fine clothing and extravagant jewelry. She is said to have power over the sexual attraction of all creatures, which is why she is also the goddess of fertility.

Yoruba myths describe Oshun as a protector and nurturer of humanity. Stories speak about the time in which Olorun sent all the orishas to revive the world and save the humans. Oshun was the one who managed to bring life back to Earth with her powerful waters. These stories claim that life on Earth would not have been possible without Oshun's intervention. Other myths portray Oshun as the wife of Shango, the orisha of thunder, and the favorite of Olorun.

Besides her sweet and nurturing nature, Oshun is also a capricious orisha. She is not a stranger to jealousy, vanity, and spite. When displeased, she is known to deprive humans of her waters, causing droughts and famine. Only when she is appeased does she revert to her kind side and become the savior of humanity.

The Yoruba people believe that Oshun is the protector of the Oshogbo village. Legends speak about the early days of humanity when Oshun allowed people to create a city near her river and promised them protection as long as they would worship her religiously. This story led to the inauguration of the annual Oshun festival that still takes place today. Every year, the Yoruba people go to the Oshun River to pay their respects and ask for good fortune. Her most devout worshipers are women, especially those who have trouble conceiving.

Fun fact about Oshun:

- She is known for her very adventurous love life. Stories speak of her numerous lovers and her short temper. When she found a suitor annoying, Oshun would turn herself into a river to avoid the interaction.
- Her favorite offerings are honey, pumpkins, coconut, spinach, almonds yams, cinnamon, lemons, chicken, and Goldschlager Liquor.
- She has a particular dislike for poisons, knives, and beer.
- Her colors are orange, golden yellow, coral, and green.
- You can create an altar for her with a yellow candle, cinnamon, anise, pumpkins and some honey which are usually kept in the bedroom.

Chicken Xinxim

Ingredients:

8 Boneless Skinless Chicken Thighs
2 teaspoons Olive Oil
1 seeded, chopped Tomato
1 chopped White Onion
1 chopped Cilantro
1 teaspoon Dende Oil or Peanut Oil
2 tablespoons Coconut Milk
1 minced Garlic Clove
1 tablespoon Lemon Juice

1 teaspoon finely chopped Peanuts

Instructions

Cut boneless chicken thighs into 2-inch chunks and brown with olive oil in skillet for 6 to 8 minutes. Add cilantro, garlic, tomato, onion, dende or peanut oil, coconut milk and lemon juice. Sprinkle with ground peanuts. Cook over low heat 25 minutes before serving hot.

Note: Can be served with white or brown rice

Oshun Mango Salsa

Ingredients:

2 pitted, peeled and diced Mangos
1/4 cup crushed Pineapple
4 chopped and seeded Tomatoes
1 diced Red Onion
1 seeded and chopped Yellow Pepper
1 clove, minced Garlic
3 tablespoon Lime Juice
¼ cup chopped Cilantro
¼ cup chopped Parsley
½ teaspoon Salt
1 tablespoon Vinegar

Directions:

Combine all ingredients together in a large bowl. Wrap or Cover and refrigerate at one hour or more before serving. Serve over grilled tuna, salmon, chicken or pork. In addition, use as a dip for tortilla chips crackers, or veggies.

Pumpkin Pie for Oshun

The Crust

Ingredients:

1 ¼ cups All-Purpose Flour
¼ cup cold Solid Shortening or Non-Salted Butter

¼ teaspoon Salt

¼ cup of Iced Water

Directions:

Make piecrust by combining the flour and salt. Cut the shortening into the flour/salt. Add the cold water one tablespoon at a time. Mix dough and repeat up until the dough is moist enough to hold it together.

With your lightly floured hands, form dough into a ball. Using a lightly floured board, roll the dough out to about 1/8 inch thickness. With a sharp knife, cut dough 1 ½ inches larger than a 9-inch pie pan turned upside-down. Gently roll the dough around the rolling pin and transfer it right side up onto the pie pan. Unroll, sliding dough into the bottom of the pie pan.

It is important to bake the crust for about 10 minutes using pie weights to keep the piecrust from puffing.

Filling

Ingredients:

2 Eggs

2 cups steamed and mashed Fresh Pumpkin

¾ cup Brown Sugar

1 ½ cup Evaporated Milk

2 tablespoons melted Butter

½ teaspoon Salt

¾ teaspoon Cinnamon

½ teaspoon Ground Ginger

1/8 teaspoon Ground Nutmeg

Directions:

Preheat oven to 400 degrees F.

Beat pumpkin in a large bowl with evaporated milk, eggs, brown sugar, cinnamon, nutmeg, ginger, and salt with a stand or electric mixer. Mix well, creating a smooth mixture. Pour into your readied crust. Bake for 40 minutes or until you can insert a toothpick in the center and it comes out clean.

Oshun's Butternut Squash Soup

Ingredients:

3 cups peeled and cubed Butternut Squash
2 cups Chicken Broth
½ minced Vidalia Onion
2 tablespoon Margarine or Butter
¼ cup Cream
¼ cup Applesauce
½ teaspoon Onion Powder
½ teaspoon Parsley
¼ teaspoon Ground Sage
Pinch Ground Cinnamon
Pinch Ground Nutmeg
Salt and Pepper to taste
2 Sauce Pans

Garnish

Pumpkin Seeds or Sunflower Seeds
Sage Sprig

Directions:

Melt butter in saucepan over low heat. Place minced onion in pan and simmer until they start to lose their color. In the other pan put in butternut squash and cover it with water. Bring to a boil and cook until the butternut squash is soft and tender. Drain, mash then add it to pan with onions. Add applesauce, chicken broth, and the spices. Combine completely and to simmer continuously over low heat for about ten minutes stirring from time to time. Take away from heat, mixing in cream, and add salt and pepper to taste. Serve with pumpkin seeds or sunflower seeds and a sprig of sage as a garnish.

Oshun Honey Pound Cake

Ingredients:

2 sticks Butter, softened

1 1/3 cups Sugar

¼ cup Honey

5 large Eggs

2 teaspoons Vanilla Extract

1 ¾ cups Flour, sifted

1 teaspoon Baking Powder

½ teaspoon Salt

Directions:

Preheat oven to 325 degrees F.

Lightly oil a 6-cup loaf pan. Beat the butter, sugar, and honey together using a mixer set on high until very light and fluffy--about 3 minutes. Beat in the eggs, one at a time. Add the vanilla extract. Add the flour, baking powder, and salt and beat until smooth.

Spoon into the prepared pan and bake until a skewer inserted into the center of the cake comes out clean--about 1 hour. Cool 15 minutes before unmolding.

Sweet Baked Oranges for Oshun

Ingredients:

6 Oranges

2 pounds Sweet Potatoes

1 cup softened, divided Butter

1 cup chopped Pecans

1 cup White Sugar

1 cup Brown Sugar

¼ cup Orange Juice

2 lightly beaten Eggs

1 tablespoon grated Orange Peel

1 teaspoon Vanilla Extract

½ teaspoon All-Purpose Flour

Directions:

Preheat the oven to 350 degrees F.

Peel the sweet potatoes, boil them until they are soft, and then mash well. Cut the tops off the six oranges removing the pulp and leaving behind only the orange shells.

In a large bowl combine sweet potatoes, orange juice, sugar, eggs, vanilla extract, ½ cup butter and grated orange peel. Spoon the mixture into orange shells, packing it well. Place in a deep casserole dish.

In a saucepan, blend the remaining ½ cup butter, brown sugar, flour and pecans over medium heat. Cook until the sugar dissolves into melted butter. Spoon mixture over the filled oranges. Add enough water to casserole dish to reach one fourth up the sides of the oranges. Bake for 30 minutes.

Pumpkin Custard

Ingredients:

24 ounces Solid-Pack Pumpkin

3 Eggs

1 ½ cup Half-And-Half Cream

1 cup packed Brown Sugar

2 teaspoons Pumpkin Pie Spice

½ teaspoon Salt

1 ½ cup of Caramel

Directions:

Preheat oven to 350 degrees.

Mix all the ingredients except caramel together. Pour into six greased 10-oz. custard cups. Place in a 13x9 baking pan; add enough hot water to reach halfway up the sides of the cups. Next, bake uncovered for 20 minutes or until set and browned lightly. Move the custards to a wire rack to cool.

Cool and serve to Oshun with caramel dripping over it.

Sweet Prosperity Oat Cakes

Ingredients:

1 ½ cups Oats
½ cup Warm Water
¼ cup Honey
¼ cup Sugar
Handful Raisins adding up to a multiple of three
1 teaspoon Vanilla Extract
½ teaspoon Pumpkin Pie Spice
½ teaspoon Salt
Almond Flakes or Breadcrumbs
Milk or Water
Coconut, Sunflower Seed or Olive Oil

Directions:

Soak the raisins until they soften. This usually takes about 20 minutes. Discard any excess water. Add all the dry ingredients followed by milk or water. If it gets too runny, add more oats. Let them sit as you do the prayers. Shape the dough into patties, and then coat them in the extra oats or seeds. Fry until golden brown.

Savory Prosperity Oat Cakes

Ingredients:

1 ½ cups Oats
1 teaspoon Salt
½ teaspoon Basil
½ teaspoon Oregano
¼ teaspoon Black Pepper
¼ teaspoon Red Pepper or Paprika
Almond Flakes or Breadcrumbs
Milk or Water
Coconut, Sunflower Seed or Olive Oil

Directions:

Add all the dry ingredients followed by milk or water. If it gets too runny, add more oats. Let them sit as you do the prayers. Shape the dough into patties, and then coat them in the extra oats or seeds. Fry until golden brown.

Note: You can add a bit of finely shredded cheese, onion, or garlic.

Chekete

Ingredients:

½ gallon Corn Liquor

8 ounce Bitter Orange

1 quart Molasses

1 gallon size Dark Colored Glass Bottle

Directions:

Put all ingredients in a bottle and leave for six months. The mixture must be stored in dark colored glass bottles and tightly sealed. It is should be covered and kept in a dark place until it ferments. After fermented it may be sweeten with honey or with cane syrup.

NINE

Extra Recipes

Ochosi's Roasted Sweet Potato Fries

Ingredients:

5 Sweet Potatoes

1 tablespoon French Fries Seasoning

½ teaspoon Paprika

Olive Oil

French Fries Seasoning:

1 cup Salt

¼ cup Black Pepper

¼ cup Garlic and Onion Powder Mixture

Directions:

Preheat oven to 450 degrees F.

After scrubbing clean, peel and slice sweet potatoes into ¼ inch long slices, then ¼ wide inch strips cover a sheet tray with parchment. In a large bowl, mix sweet potatoes with just enough oil to coat. Sprinkle with French Fries Seasoning and paprika. Place sweet potatoes in single layer on a readied baking sheet, making sure not to overcrowd. Turnings occasionally, bake until sweet potatoes are tender and golden brown, about 20 minutes. Let cool 5 to 10 minutes before serving.

You may also place them in a large bowl and give them to Ochosi as a cooked offering. Remove sweet potatoes after a suitable amount of time and get rid of them in natural settings as determined by means of insight.

Baked Sweet Potatoes

Ingredients:

6 medium unpeeled Sweet Potatoes
6 tablespoons Unsalted Butter
½ teaspoon Salt
1/8 teaspoon Black Pepper

Directions:

Preheat oven to 400 degrees F.

Perforate each sweet potato numerous times with the tines of a fork. Place the sweet potatoes on a border edged baking sheet lined with foil. Bake, about 45 minutes until tender. Create a slit in the top of each sweet potato. Top with 1 tablespoon of butter and season with the salt and pepper.

Orunmila's Golden Yams Brownies

Ingredients:

2 cups peeled and finely shredded Yam
1 ½ cups All-Purpose Flour
1 cup Confectioners' Sugar
1 cup Butter
1 cup packed Brown Sugar
1 cup White Sugar
4 Eggs
2 tablespoons Butter or Margarine
2 tablespoons Milk
2 teaspoons Vanilla Extract

1 teaspoon Baking Powder

½ teaspoon Salt

Directions:

Preheat oven to 350 degrees F. Grease a 9x13 inch baking dish.

In a large bowl, cream the butter, white sugar, and brown sugar together until smooth. Beat the eggs in one at a time, and then stir in the vanilla. Combine the flour, baking powder, and salt; stir into the batter until blended. Fold in the shredded yam. Once combined, pour batter evenly in the greased baking dish.

Bake for 30 minutes in the preheated oven, or until a toothpick can be inserted into the center, coming out clean. Mix the confectioners' sugar, butter and milk until smooth. Spread mixture over the brownies while they are still warm. Can be served hot or warm.

Tembleque Coconut Pudding

Ingredients:

2 14 ounce cans Coconut Milk

¾ cup Sugar

½ cup Cornstarch

¼ teaspoon Salt

Pinch Ground Cinnamon

Directions:

Mix coconut milk, sugar, and salt together in a saucepan. Spoon a few tablespoons of the coconut milk mixture into a small bowl and stir cornstarch into the mixture to dissolve. Pour into the mixture in the saucepan. Bring the mixture to a boil while stirring continuously. Cook about 5 minutes until thick and smooth.

Pour the coconut milk mixture into molds, covering each with plastic wrap. Refrigerate until cold and firm, which may take 3 hours to 2 days.

Run a thin knife around the edges of the mold and turn upside down onto a plate to remove. Decorate the tops with cinnamon.

Sweet Potato Pudding

Ingredients:

2 to 3 medium Sweet Potatoes
4 large Eggs
½ cup packed Light or Dark Brown Sugar
1/3 cup Milk
2 tablespoons melted Unsalted Butter
1 tablespoon Pure Vanilla Extract
1 tablespoon Dark Corn Syrup
2 teaspoons Grated Orange Peel
½ teaspoon Ground Cinnamon
½ teaspoon Ground Ginger
½ teaspoon Salt

Directions:

Preheat the oven to 350 degrees F. Grease a 1 ½ quart-baking dish.

Scrub and pierce sweet potatoes with the tines of a fork. Bake at 350 degrees for 1 to 1 ¼ hours or until very tender. Cut sweet potatoes in half; scoop out flesh and place in a large bowl. Mush with milk and egg. Stir in the brown sugar vanilla, orange peel and salt until blended.

Using an electric mixer beat together all the pudding ingredients until smooth and light. Pour the pudding into the baking dish coated with cooking spray. Move it to the oven and bake for 25 minutes.

Praline Topping

Ingredients:

½ cup chopped Pecans

¼ cup chopped crystallized Ginger

¼ cup packed Dark or Light Brown Sugar

2 tablespoons softened Unsalted Butter

Directions:

In a small bowl, combine the ingredients and store to use as the topping for sweet potato pudding. After Sprinkling the praline mixture over the pudding, bake for an additional 20 to 25 minutes, or until the pudding is set and slightly puffed. Do not worry; the top will drop as the pudding cools. Cool on a wire rack for 1 hour. Serve warm or at room temperature. Serve with whipped topping. Be sure to keep leftovers refrigerated.

Papaya Cream

Ingredients:

1 ripe Papaya

1 Scoop Vanilla Ice Cream

1 tablespoon Crème De Cassis Liqueur

Directions:

Peel papaya and take out the seeds. Cut the papaya in small pieces. Place papaya in blender with ice cream. Blend long enough until you don't have any pieces of papaya or until creamy. Be mindful not to over blend or else the ice cream will turn into more soup than creamy. Pour the Crème de Cassis, stir with a spoon and serve right away.

TEN

Yoruba Celebrations

During Yoruba festivals, the participants are partaking in ritualistic re-enactments of myths and folk stories that refer to the birth of humankind and humanity's place in the Universe. During festivals, religious beliefs are celebrated alongside family, music, dance, and heritage. It's also a time when communities forget about their differences and come together as one to help and support each other.

There are many festivals dedicated to kings, queens, orishas, and special occasions. I will cover only a few so we don't get wrapped up in too many celebrations.

Ifa Festival

The Ifa Festival is an annual seven-day Yoruba celebration. It celebrates the orisha Orunmila (also known as Ifa), and it ends on the first Saturday of June. The festival falls at the time of the yam harvest, and there are sacrifices made to Orunmila and rituals that involve the cutting of yam. These tuber vegetables are considered by the Yoruba to be symbols of thanksgiving. It is almost a sacred rule to give a yam offering to the orishas before eating the fruits of their labor.

The festival is a mixture of dancing, drumming, feasting, and religious rituals. Sacrifices are made to Ooni's oracle, rituals are performed by the Awo Oloju merindinlogun (the cult with 16 faces) and by the Arabata Agbaye (the backbone of the world) priest, and discussions on social aspects of the community take place and prayers are made.

Eyo Festival

The Eyo Festival is very popular among the Yoruba people, especially those from Lagos. The 24-day festival takes its name from the costumed dancers that perform during the celebration. The "Eyo" are dressed in white robes that cover their entire bodies; they have decorated top hats, and they hold traditional sticks. The origin of the festival is said to date back to a parade held in honor of a dead Lagos king.

The Eyo festival is a beloved tourist attraction that takes place on Lagos Island. Thanks to this celebration, the small local businesses are thriving.

Osun-Osogbo Festival

The Osun-Osogbo Festival is an annual celebration dedicated to the orisha Oshun. It takes place at the Osun-Osogbo Sacred Grove (a site that's listed as being a UNESCO World Heritage Site) in the month of August, and it lasts two weeks. The whole month of August is celebrated as one of tradition, celebration, and a time to reunite with ancestors.

Some notable events that take place during this festival are Iwopopo (the cleansing of the Osogbo town), the Ibroriade (the assembling of the crowns of past Osogbo kings), and the 3-day lighting of the 500-year-old lamp Ina Olojumerindinlogun. Prior to the celebrations, the priests vow to abstain from fighting, cursing, and eating certain foods, so Oshun will find them worthy. Offerings consisting of kola nuts, snails, pigeons, honey, and palm oil are made to appease Oshun and protect the people from her wrath.

Ojude-Oba Festival

The Ojude-Oba Festival takes place in the Yoruba town Ijebu Ode, and it celebrates the history, myths, victories, and diversity of the Ogun region. The festival is held on the third day after Eid al-Kabir, and it is attended by Yoruba people from all around Africa to celebrate with their peers and pay homage to old kings.

Olojo Festival

The Olojo Festival is an annual celebration that takes place in the central Yoruba city, Ife-Ife. It honors the orisha of iron, Ogun, who is celebrated by the Yoruba as being the first son of the legendary King Oduduwa. Popular Yoruba belief is that Olodumare, the orisha of creation, has blessed the day of the Olojo Festival, and to honor that, the Ooni (king) of Ife-Ife makes a public appearance wearing the Are Crown. The Ooni will then visit shrines and pray for peace and prosperity in Yorubaland.

This festival holds a special place in the Yoruba's hearts because it is seen as a day of unification for the Yoruba people.

The Importance of Yoruba Celebrations

The social aspect of Yoruba festivals is very apparent, especially since it's not uncommon at all for smaller celebrations such as marriages, naming ceremonies, and burials to be mixed in with the religious festival. Yoruba festivals promote cultural value and focus on protecting the heritage of the people that partake in them.

Even when the people of the community don't adhere to the same religious beliefs, they are still able to come together and celebrate both their deities and differences. At the end of the day, they all pray for the same things: mercy, blessings, and protection.

Afterword

As you can see, cooking for the Orishas is not as difficult as you may think. There are many recipes that we already enjoy that can be prepared for them as well as some that we can enjoy ourselves.

Just because they come from many countries as well as cultures, they may actually seem familiar to you and you may know them by other names.

So go ahead, slap on that apron and start cooking today. Get yourself in tuned with the Orishas. You may even notice increased positivity, prosperity and creativeness coming into your home and life.

About the Author

Monique Joiner Siedlak is a writer, witch, and warrior on a mission to awaken people to their greatest potential through the power of storytelling infused with mysticism, modern paganism, and new age spirituality. At the young age of 12, she began rigorously studying the fascinating philosophy of Wicca. By the time she was 20, she was self-initiated into the craft, and hasn't looked back ever since. To this day, she has authored over 40 books pertaining to the magick and mysteries of life.

To find out more about Monique Joiner Siedlak artistically, spiritually, and personally, feel free to visit her **official website**.

www.mojosiedlak.com

facebook.com/mojosiedlak
twitter.com/mojosiedlak
instagram.com/mojosiedlak
pinterest.com/mojosiedlak
bookbub.com/authors/monique-joiner-siedlak

More Books by Monique

Personal Growth and Development

Creative Visualization
Astral Projection for Beginners
Meditation for Beginners
Reiki for Beginners
Manifesting With the Law of Attraction
Stress Management

The Yoga Collective

Yoga for Beginners
Yoga for Stress
Yoga for Back Pain
Yoga for Weight Loss
Yoga for Flexibility
Yoga for Advanced Beginners
Yoga for Fitness
Yoga for Runners
Yoga for Energy
Yoga for Your Sex Life
Yoga: To Beat Depression and Anxiety

Yoga for Menstruation

A Natural Beautiful You

Creating Your Own Body Butter
Creating Your Own Body Scrub
Creating Your Own Body Spray

THANK YOU FOR READING MY BOOK! I REALLY APPRECIATE ALL OF YOUR FEEDBACK AND I LOVE TO HEAR WHAT YOU HAVE TO SAY. PLEASE LEAVE YOUR REVIEW AT YOUR FAVORITE RETAILER!

www.ingramcontent.com/pod-product-compliance
Lightning Source LLC
Chambersburg PA
CBHW071632040426
42452CB00009B/1590

* 9 7 8 1 9 4 8 8 3 4 7 1 1 *

www.ingramcontent.com/pod-product-compliance
Lightning Source LLC
Chambersburg PA
CBHW071632040426
42452CB00009B/1590

9781948834711